TOTES

Coloring Book

by Patricia Burke

Copyright © 2019 by Patricia Burke

ALL RIGHTS RESERVED

This publication is protected by US and International Copyright Law

No part of this publication may be reproduced, reused or deconstructed for use in any other images, republished or distributed in any way or by any means existing. Including but not limited to electronic or mechanical means

ISBN- 13: 978-1-951576-02-8

Cover Art Hand Drawn by Doodle Artist Patricia Burke

Copyright © 2019 by Patricia Burke
All Rights Reserved

This publication is protected by international and USA copyright law. No part of this publication may be reproduced, reused, republished, or distributed in any form or by any means, electronic or mechanical.
This publication may not be stored in any database or retrieval system without the prior written permission of the artist and or copyright holder.

Purchaser is permitted to photocopy the original pages in this book to color for their PERSONAL USE ONLY. This personal use, means limited use and does not allow or permit mass production or selling the images contained within for commercial gain.

You may not share the images on the page within this publication with friends and or family. This limited use does not grant you the right to make multiple copies for distribution to any person, entity, social media sites, no matter how innocent the intention.

Purchaser of this publication is granted permission to share or post their personally COLORED VERSION ONLY, as long at they do not remove the copyright information from the images or pages and that they attribute the original artwork to the artist, Patricia Burke.

NO other permission is given to alter, reproduce, share, sell, transmit, post or disseminate, in part or in whole any of the pages or images in this book.
Patricia Burke would love to see your colored version of her art.
You can find her here:

http://coloradoodle.com
https://www.facebook.com/coloradoodle/
https:// www.facebook.com/groups/

Join the official fan group here;
facebook.com/groups/colormydoodles.patriciaburke

TOTES Coloring Team

Brenda Hanson

Cari McBroom Jimenez

Charlotte Schroeder Beeston

Debbie West Cummings

Kelly Deuber Taylor

Susan Nicita

Vicki Ardito

The way you put the colors
you choose to the page, wow.
You are always amazing!
Thank you. Patricia

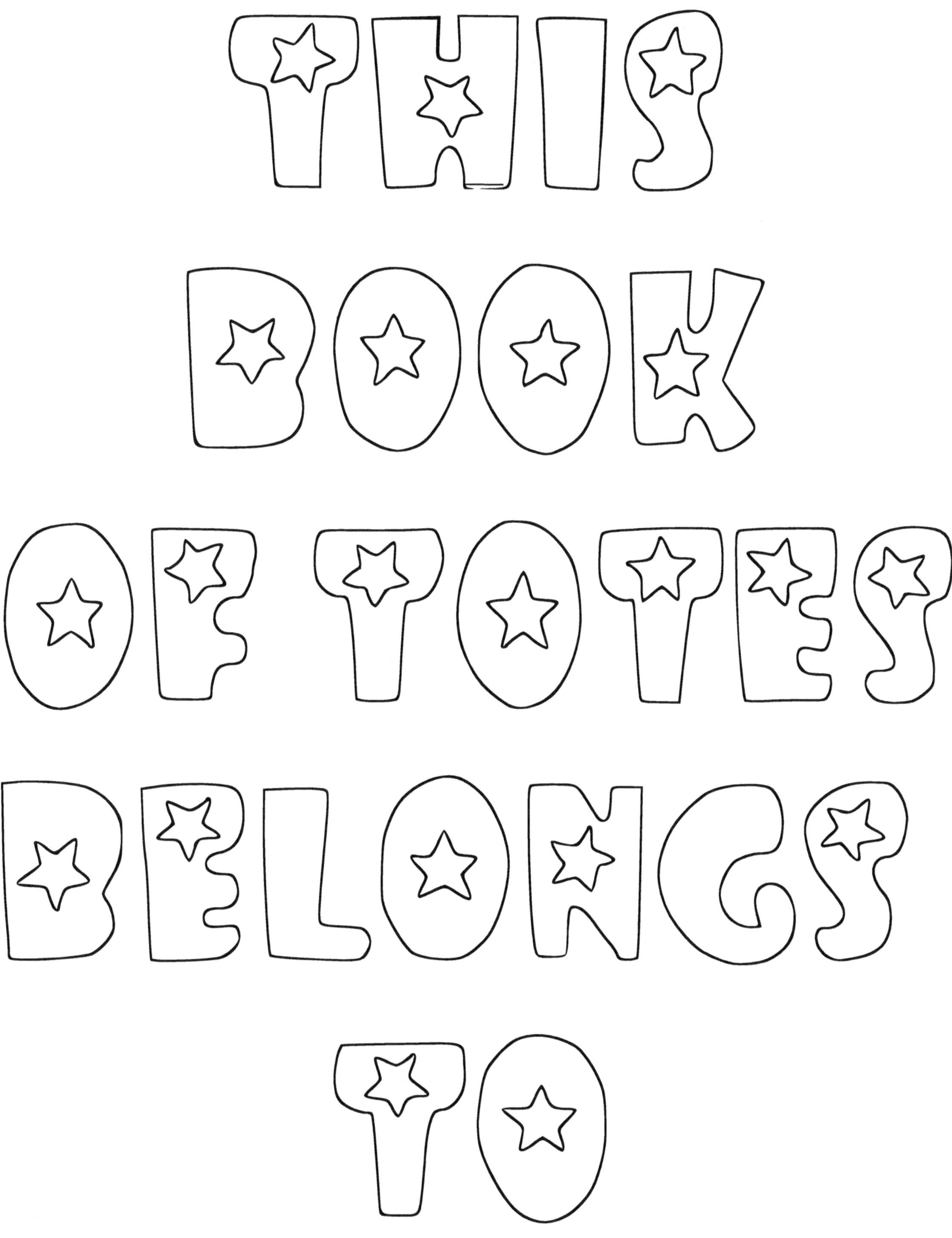
THIS
BOOK
OF TOTES
BELONGS
TO

www.coloradoodle.com Copyright 2019 Patricia Burke

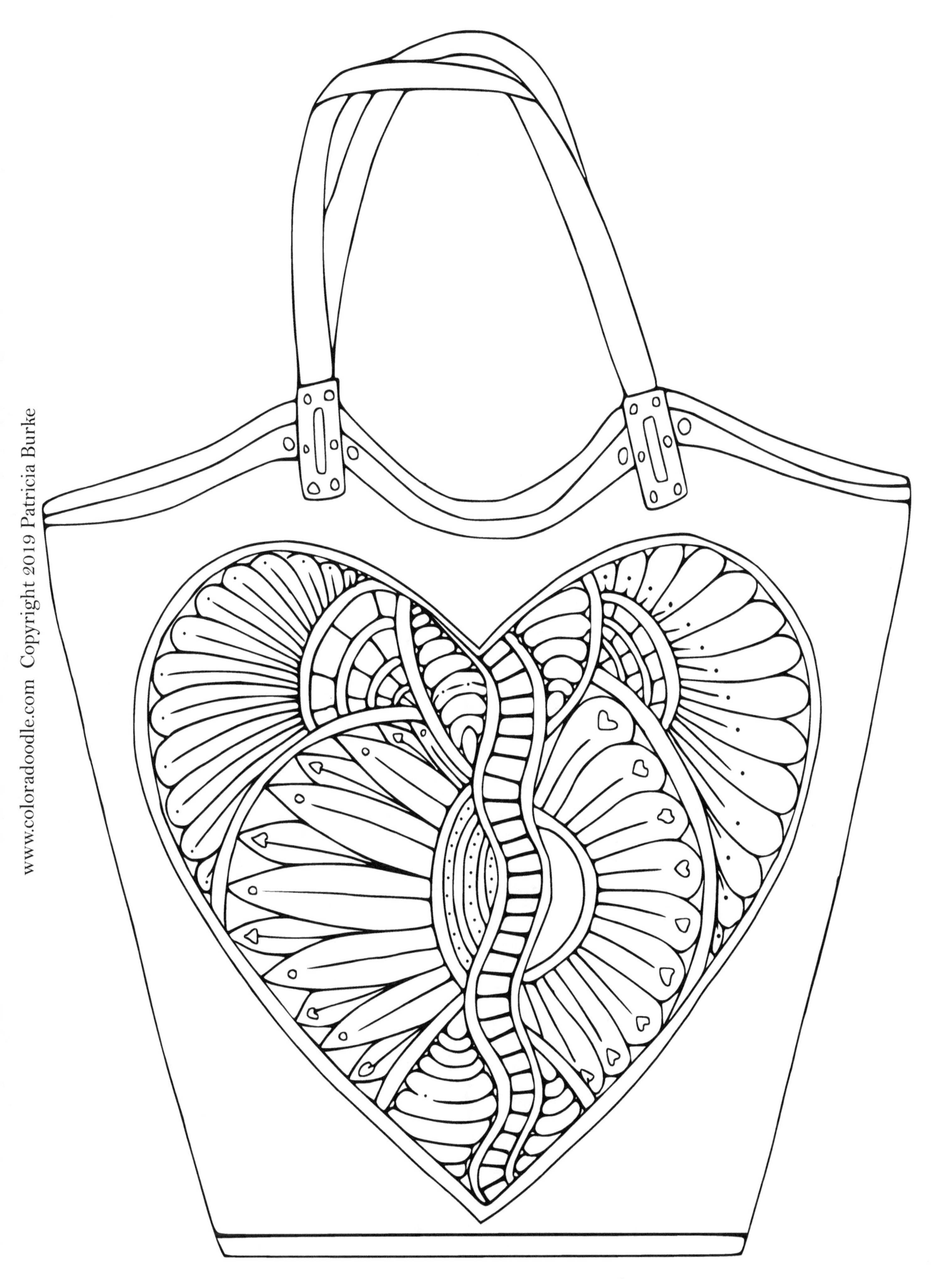

www.coloradoodle.com Copyright 2019 Patricia Burke

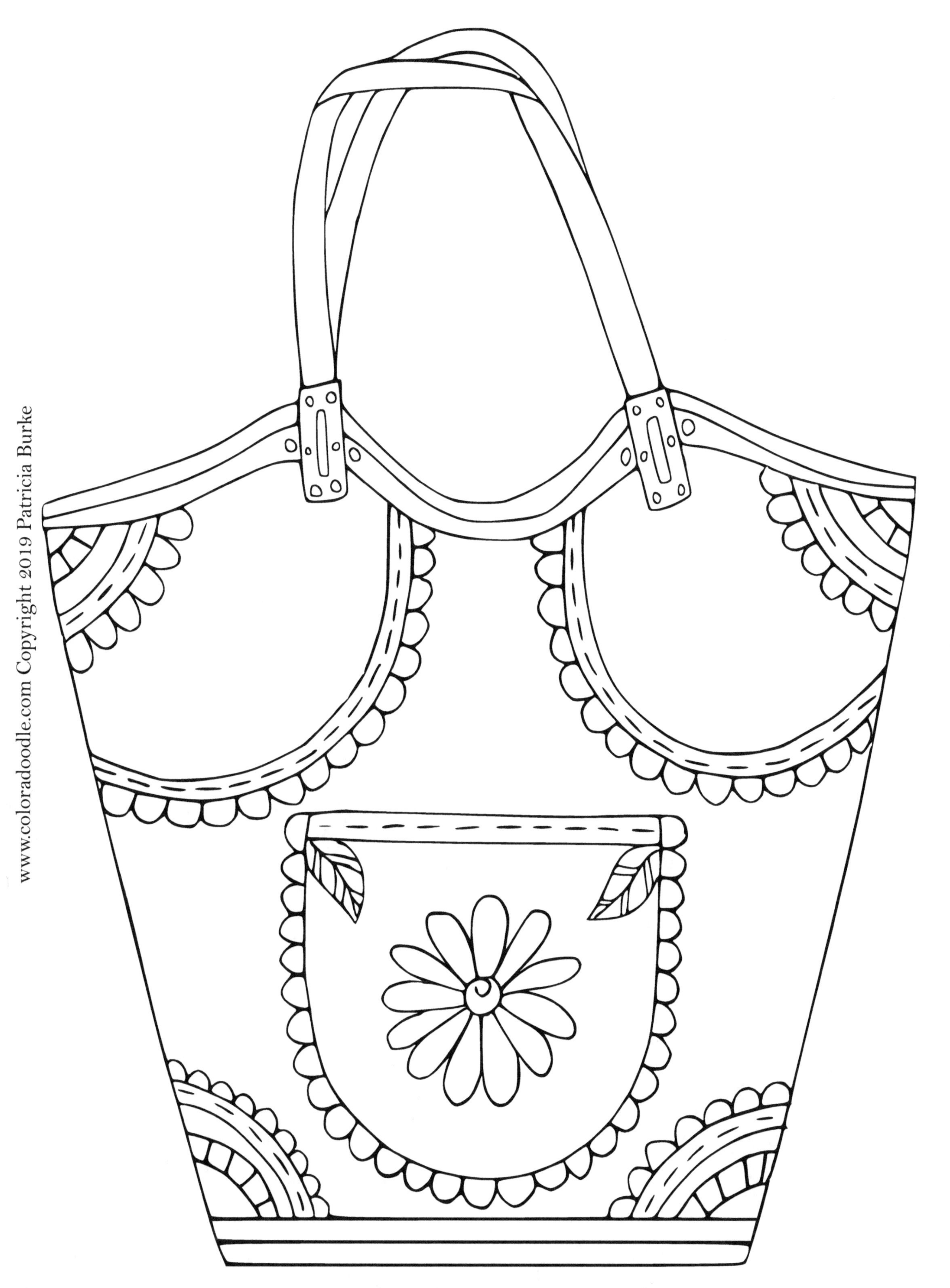

www.coloradoodle.com Copyright 2019 Patricia Burke

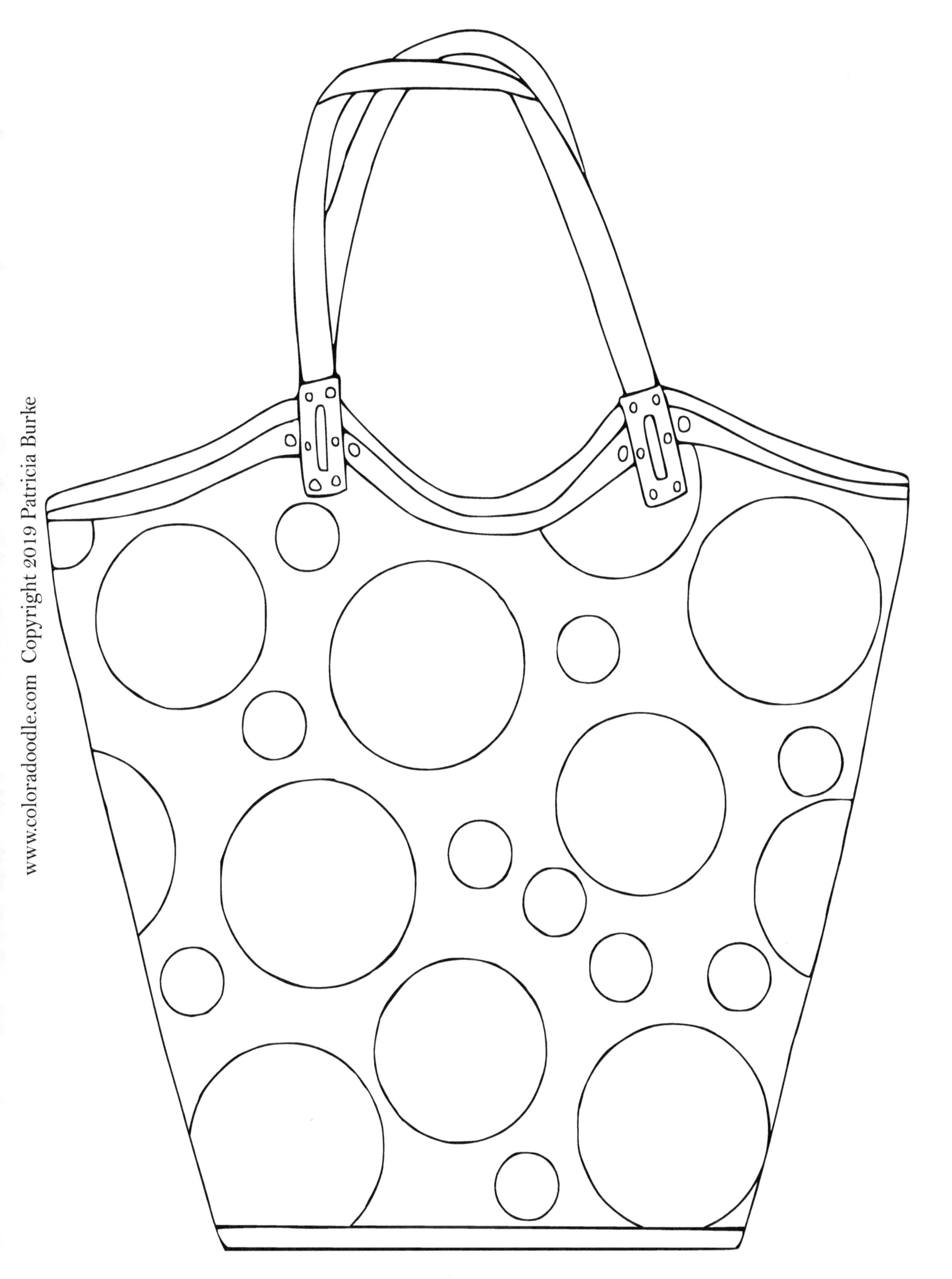

www.coloradoodle.com Copyright 2019 Patricia Burke

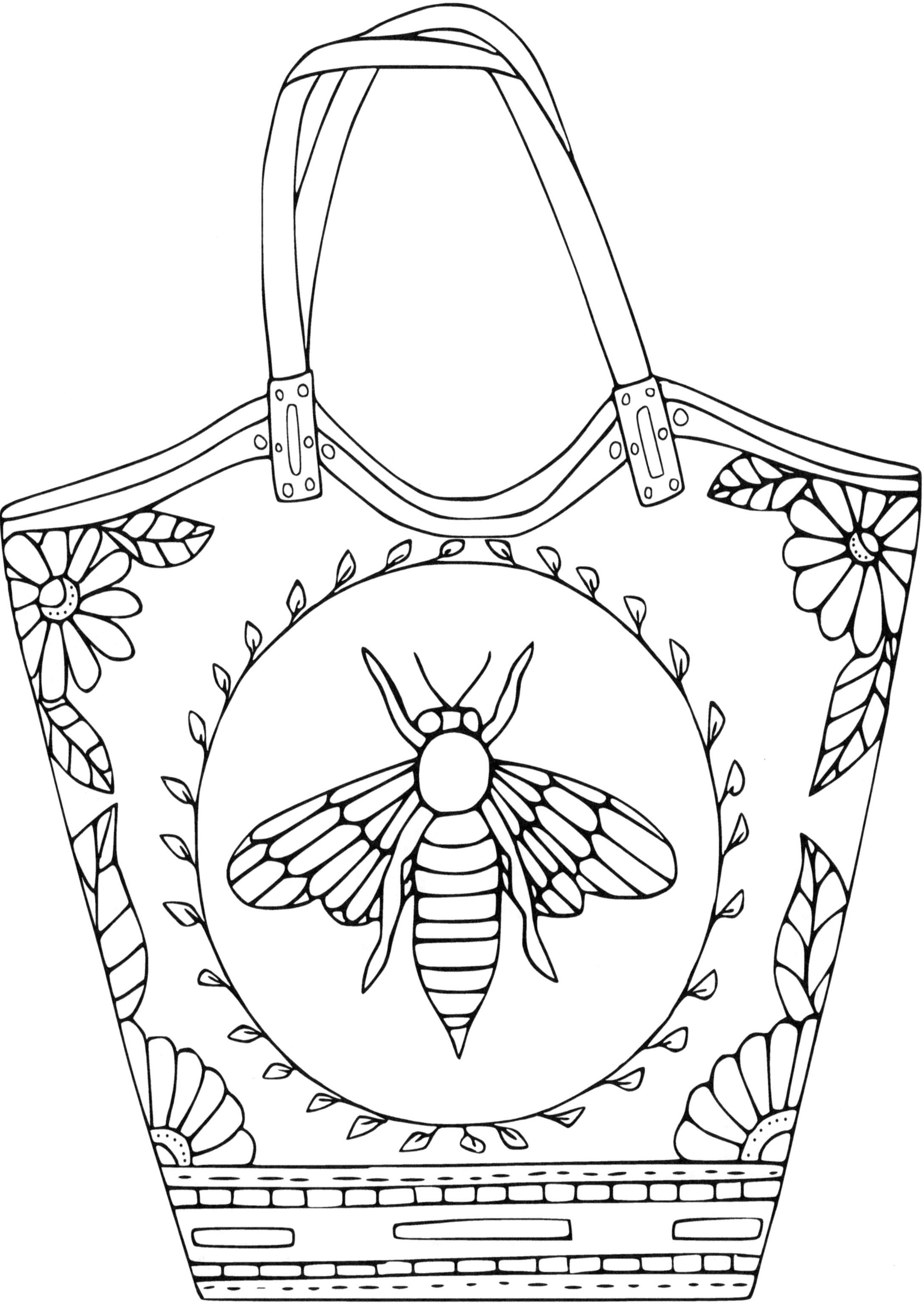

www.coloradoodle.com Copyright 2019 Patricia Burke

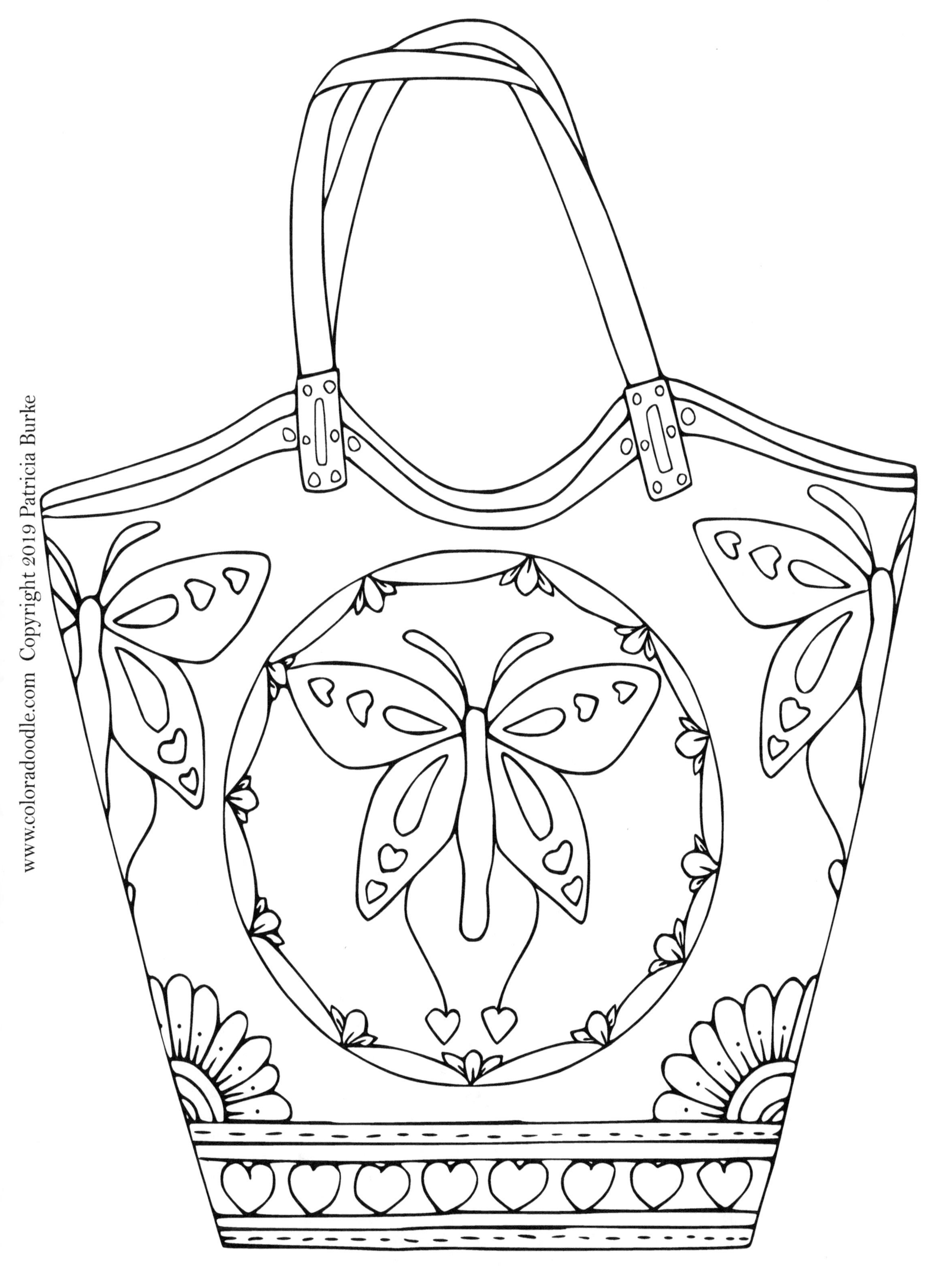
www.coloradoodle.com Copyright 2019 Patricia Burke

www.coloradoodle.com Copyright 2019 Patricia Burke

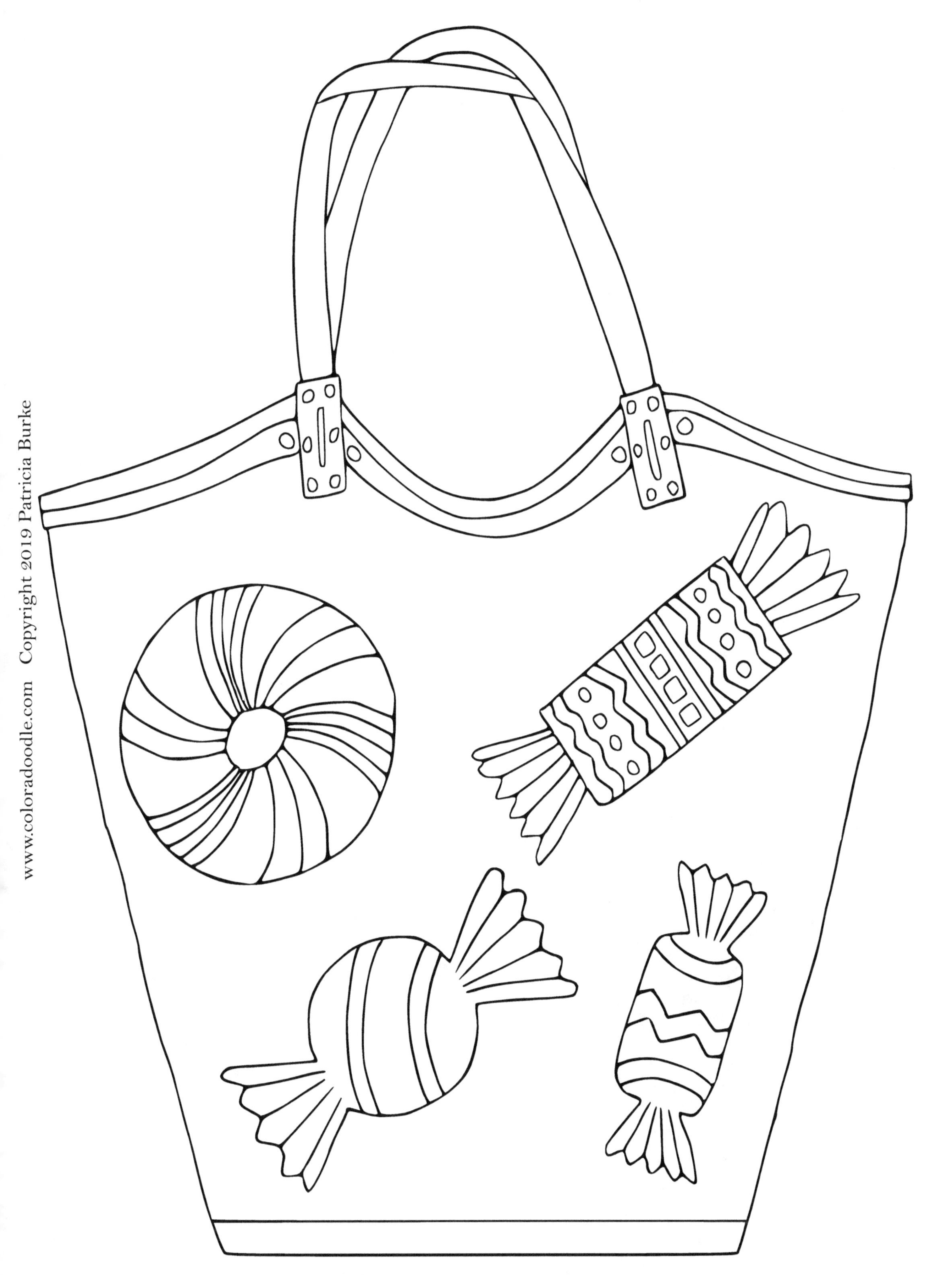

www.coloradoodle.com Copyright 2019 Patricia Burke

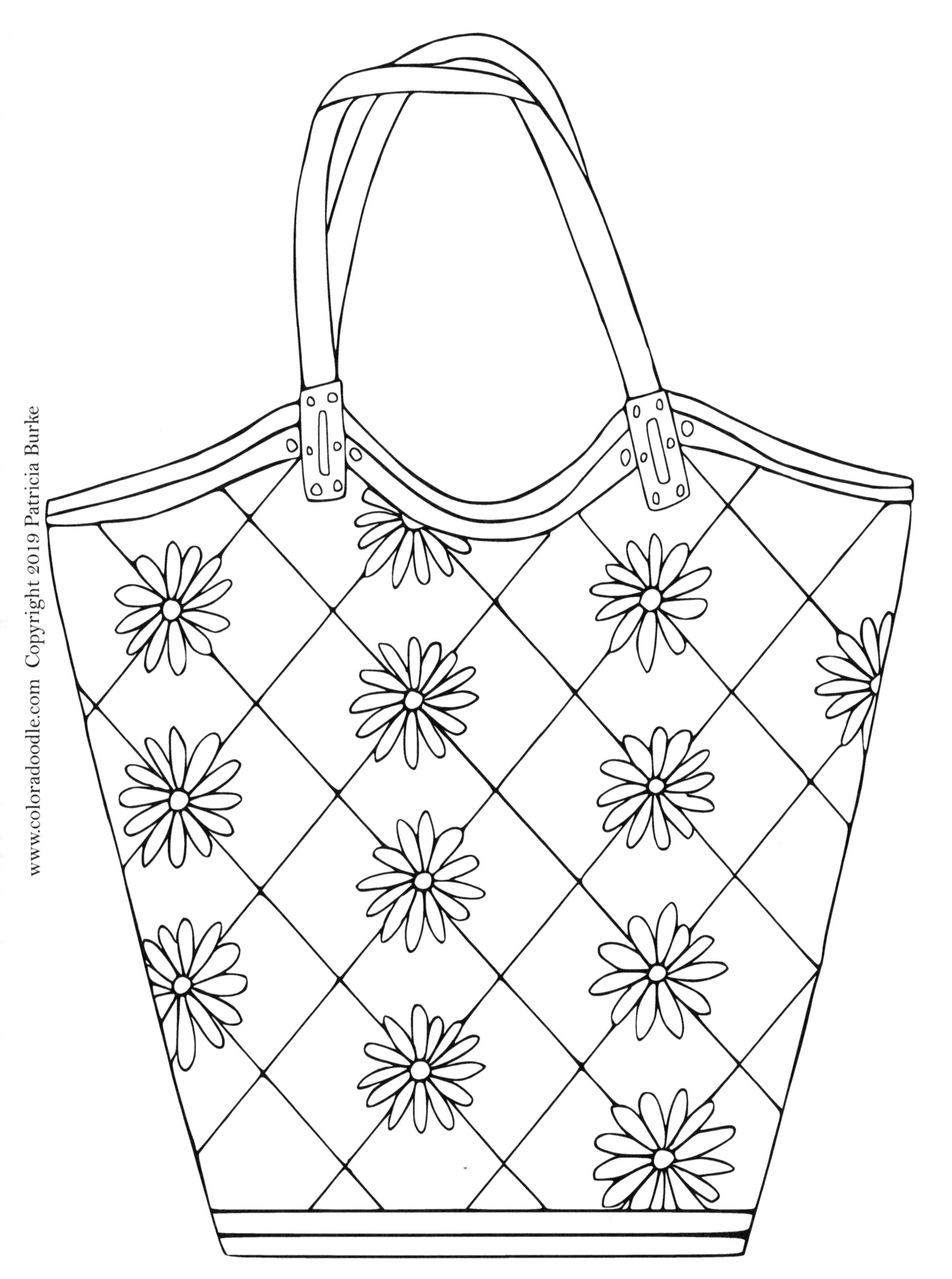

www.coloradoodle.com Copyright 2019 Patricia Burke

www.coloradoodle.com Copyright 2019 Patricia Burke

www.coloradoodle.com Copyright 2019 Patricia Burke

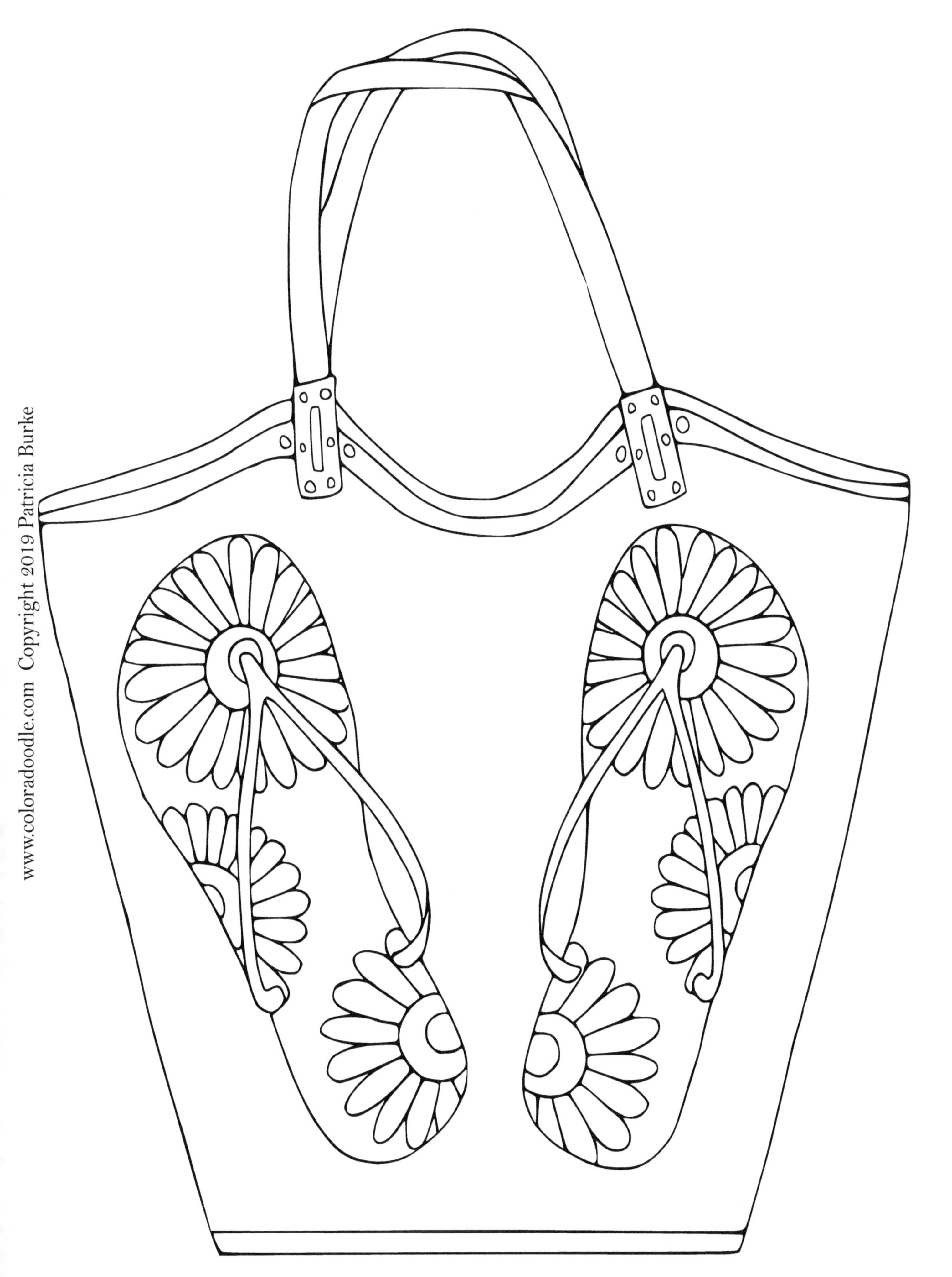

www.coloradoodle.com Copyright 2019 Patricia Burke

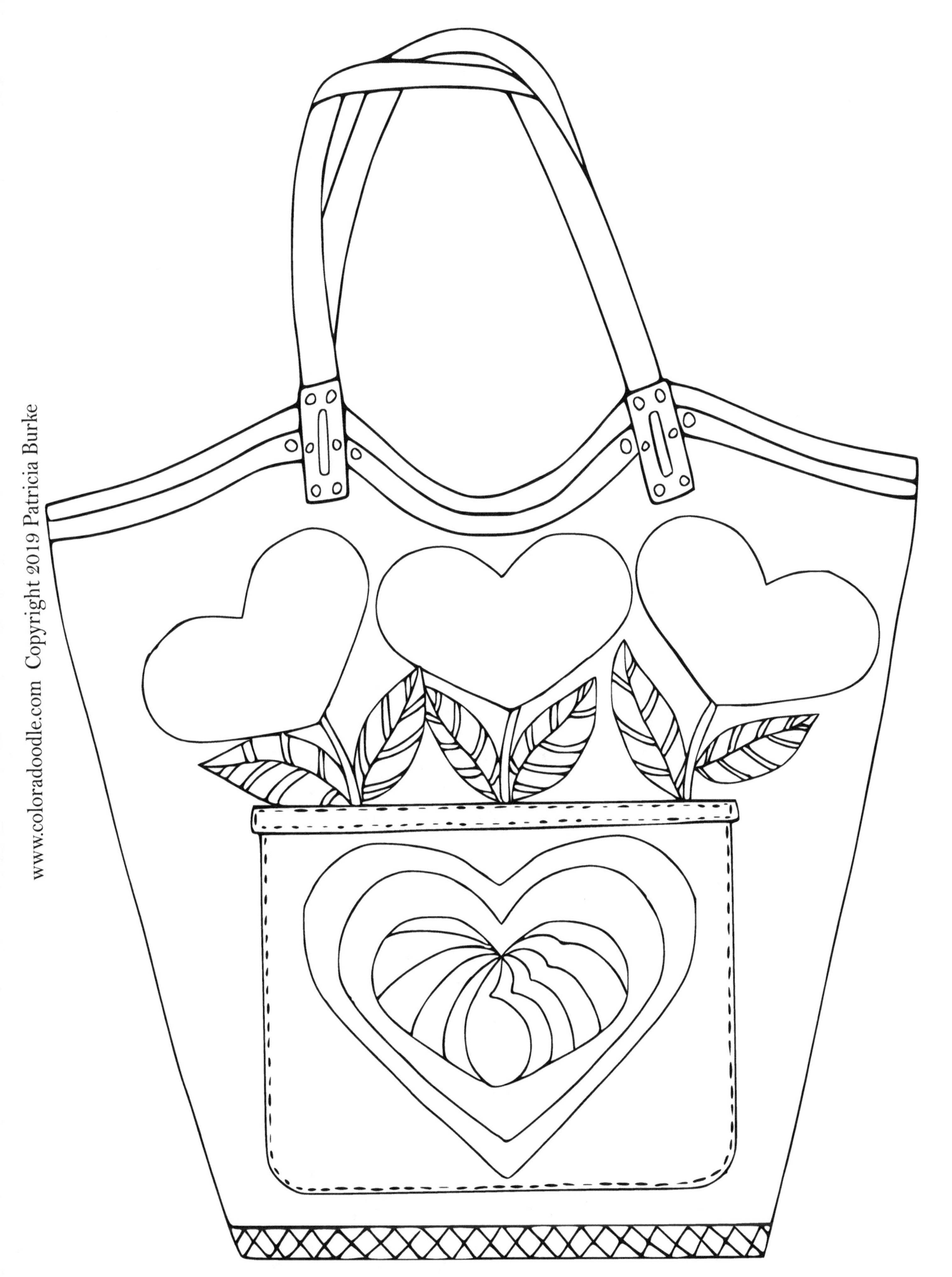

www.coloradoodle.com Copyright 2019 Patricia Burke

www.coloradoodle.com Copyright 2019 Patricia Burke

www.coloradoodle.com Copyright 2019 Patricia Burke

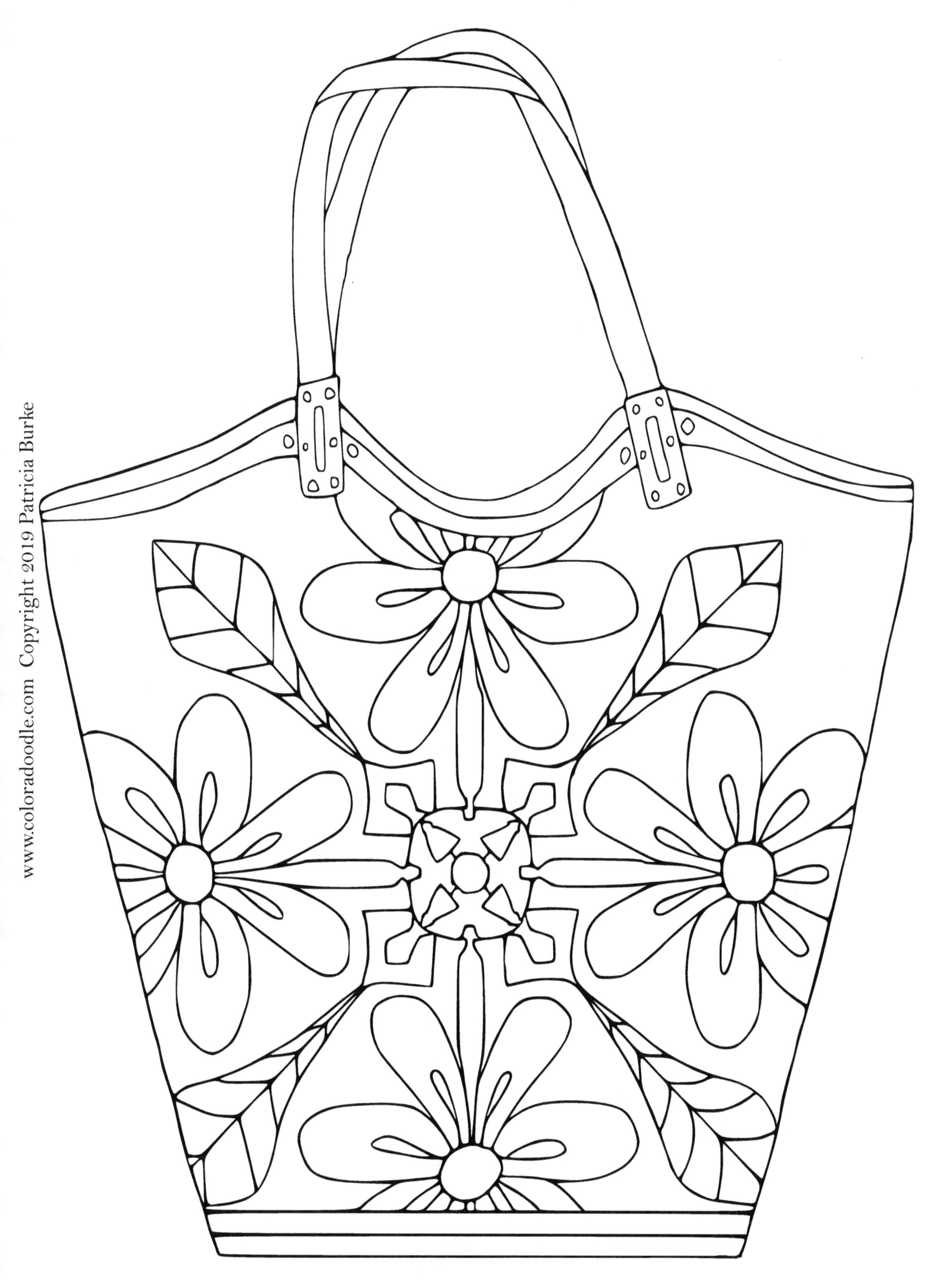

www.coloradoodle.com Copyright 2019 Patricia Burke

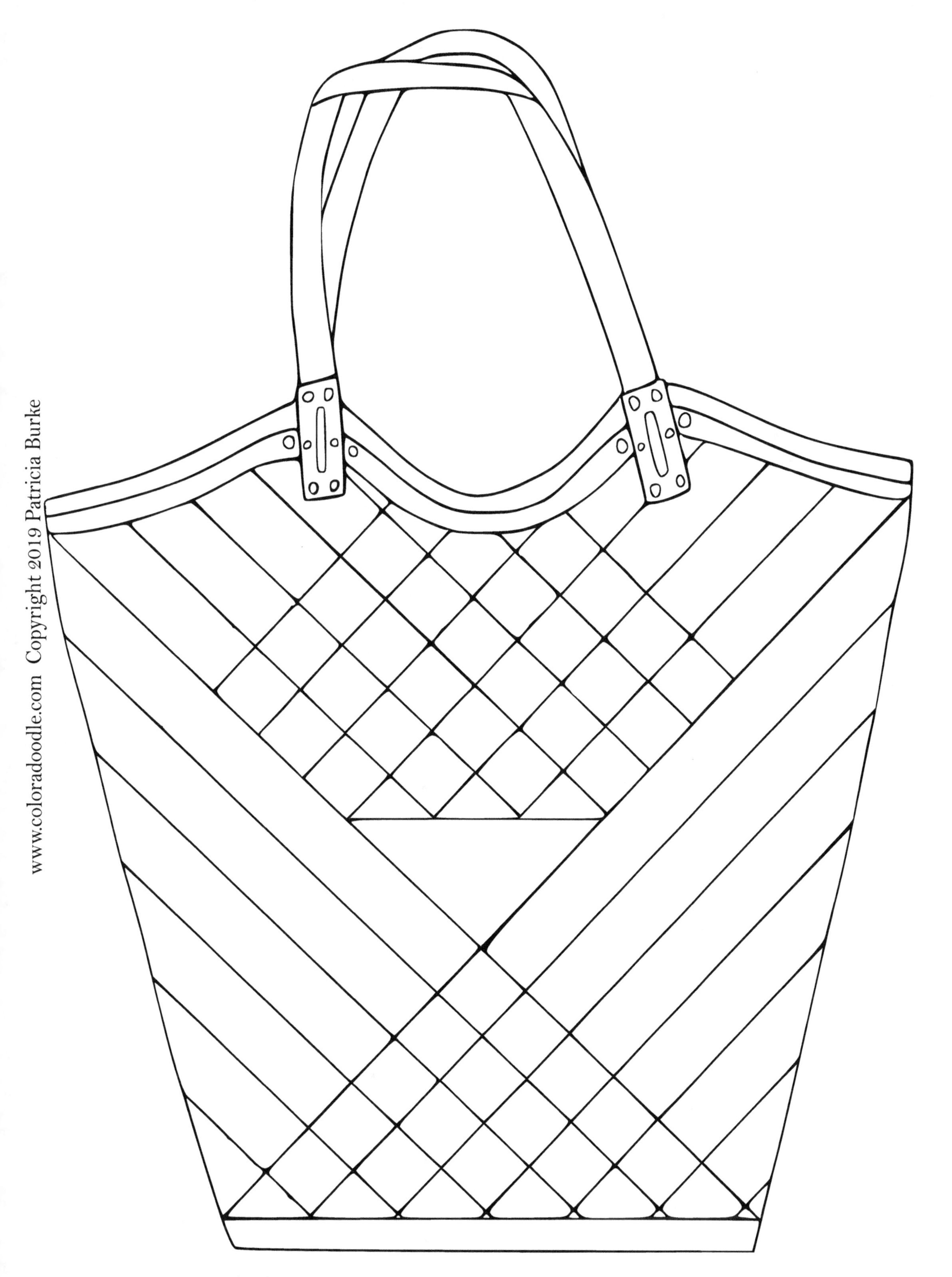

www.coloradoodle.com Copyright 2019 Patricia Burke

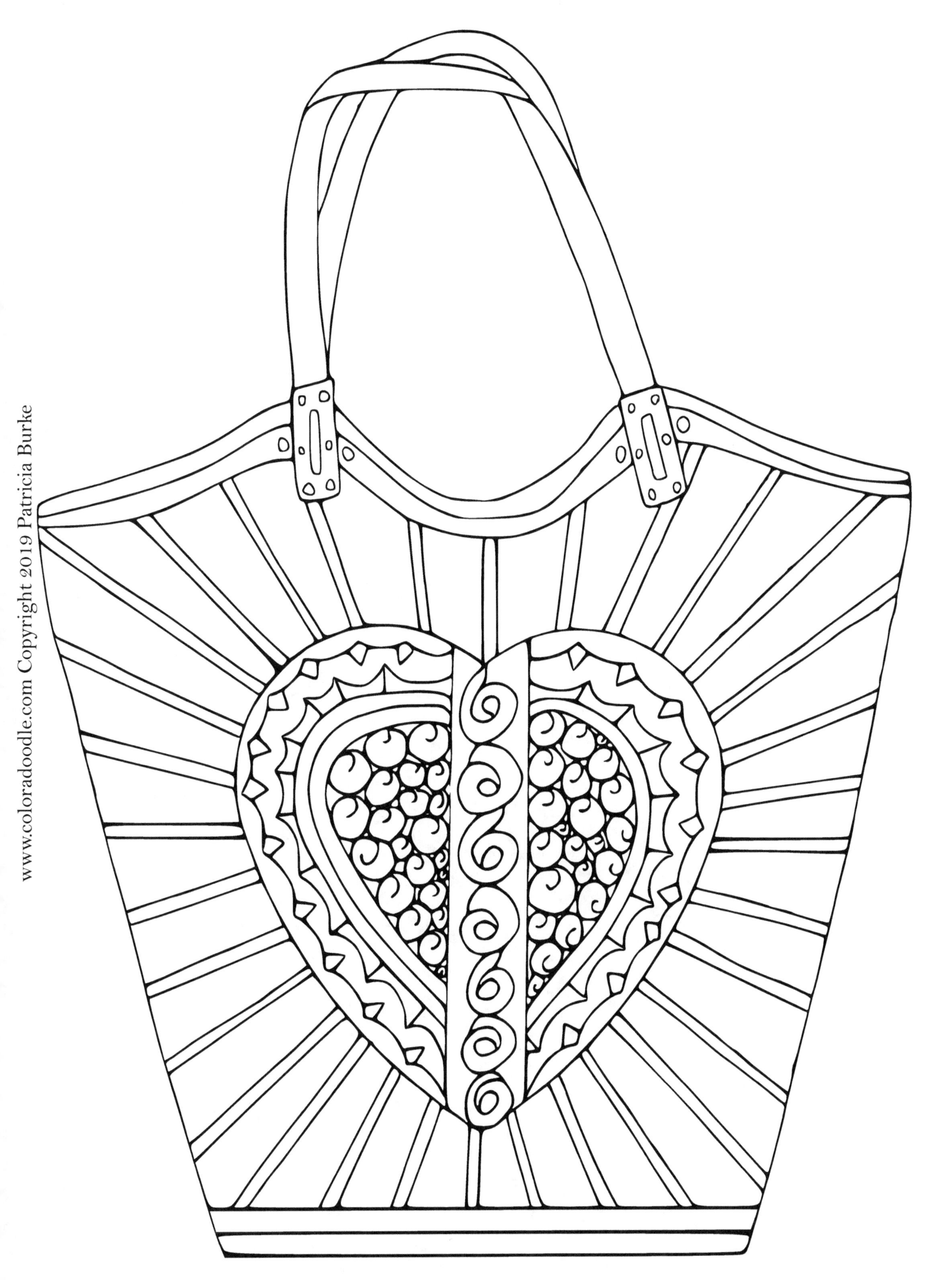

www.coloradoodle.com Copyright 2019 Patricia Burke

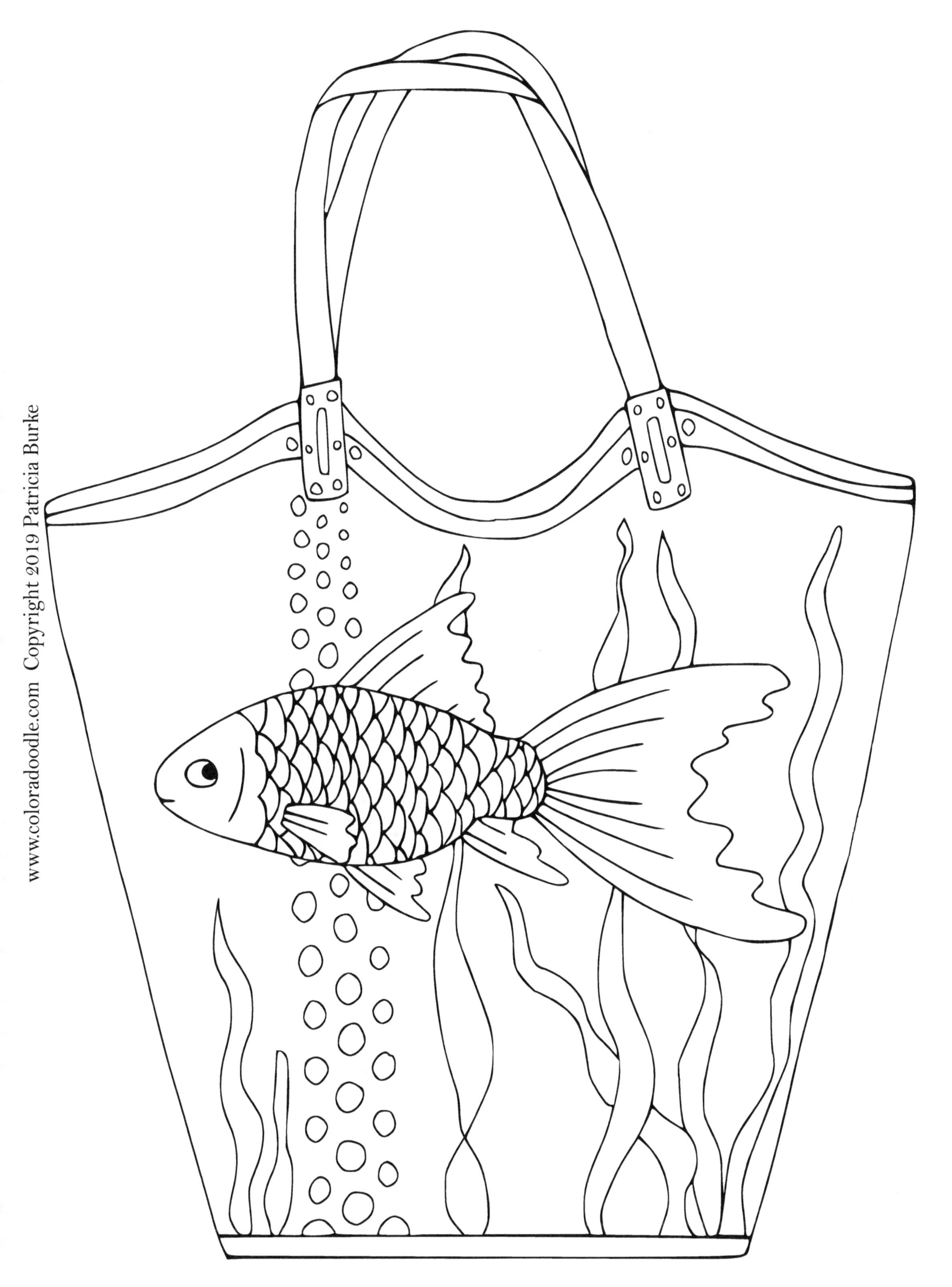

www.coloradoodle.com Copyright 2019 Patricia Burke

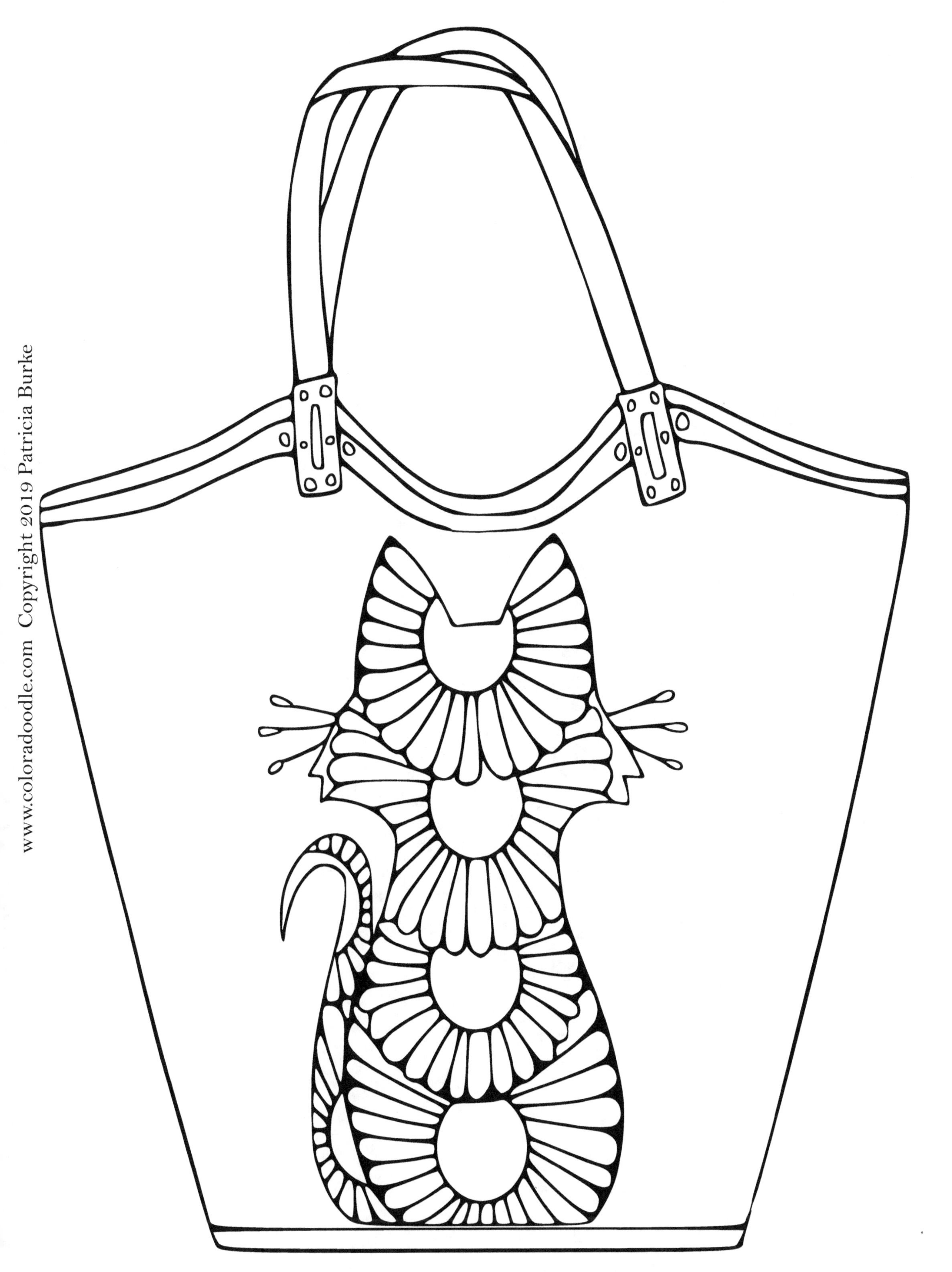

www.coloradoodle.com Copyright 2019 Patricia Burke

www.coloradoodle.com Copyright 2019 Patricia Burke

www.coloradoodle.com Copyright 2019 Patricia Burke

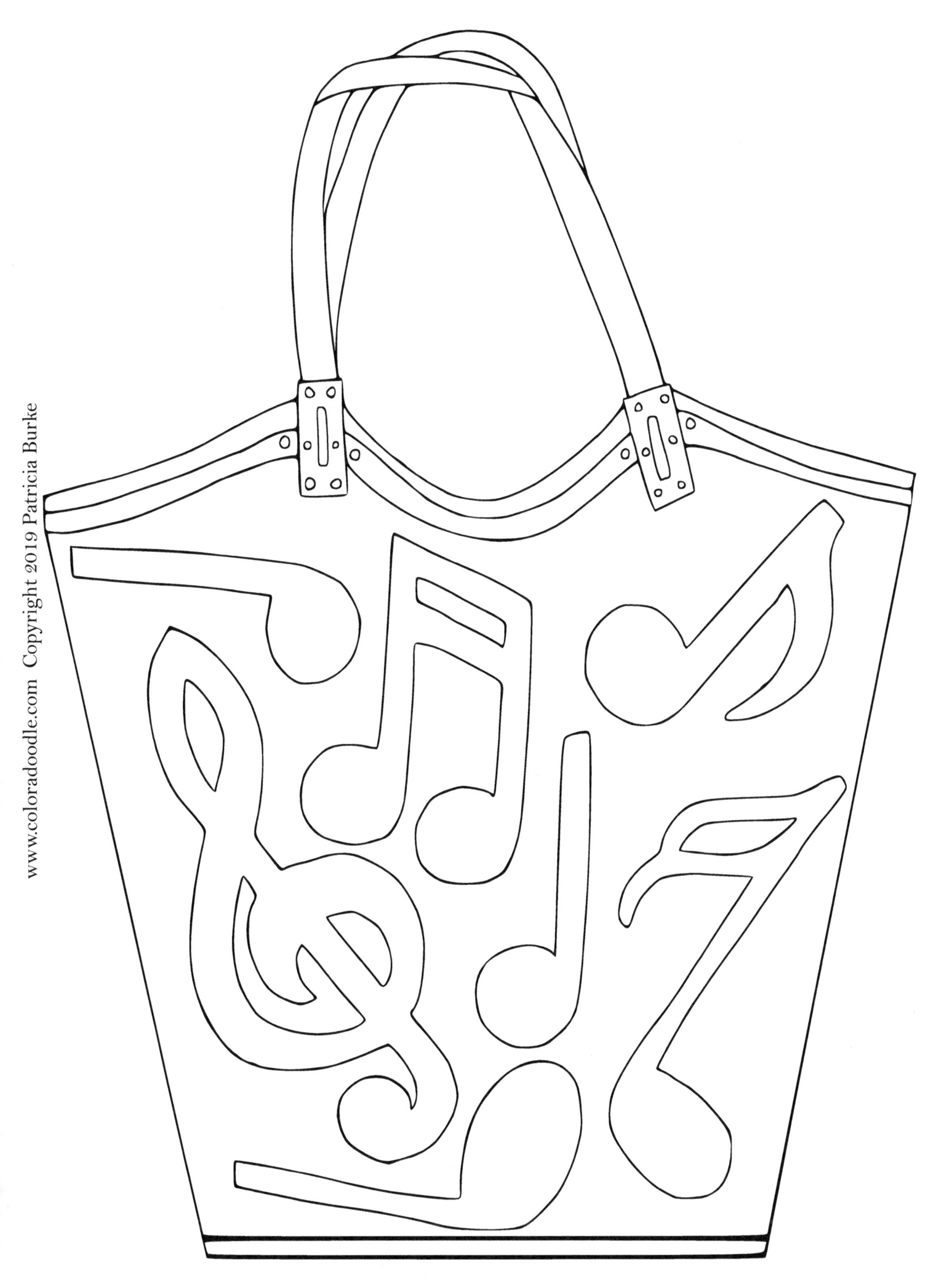

www.coloradoodle.com Copyright 2019 Patricia Burke

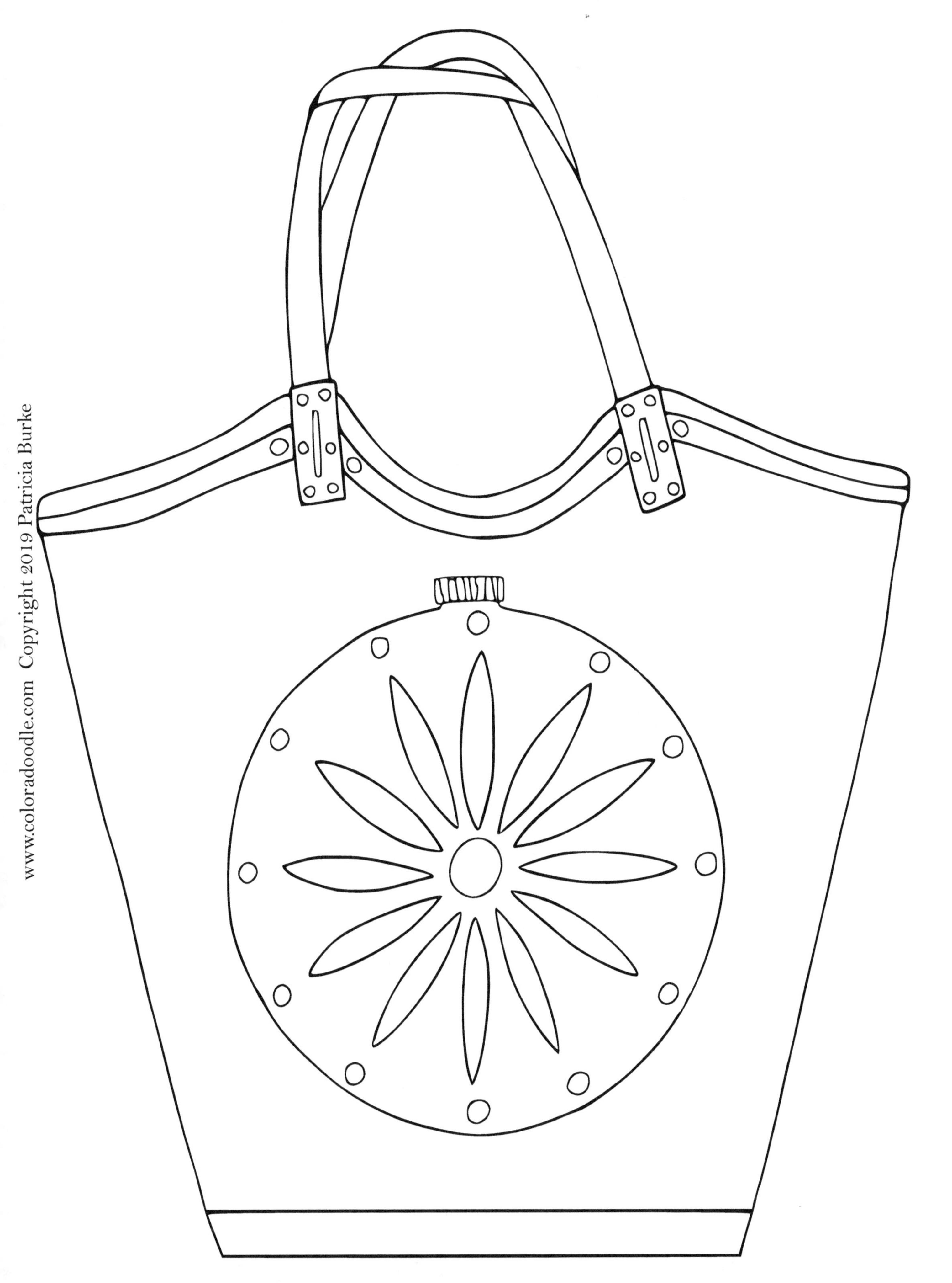

www.coloradoodle.com Copyright 2019 Patricia Burke

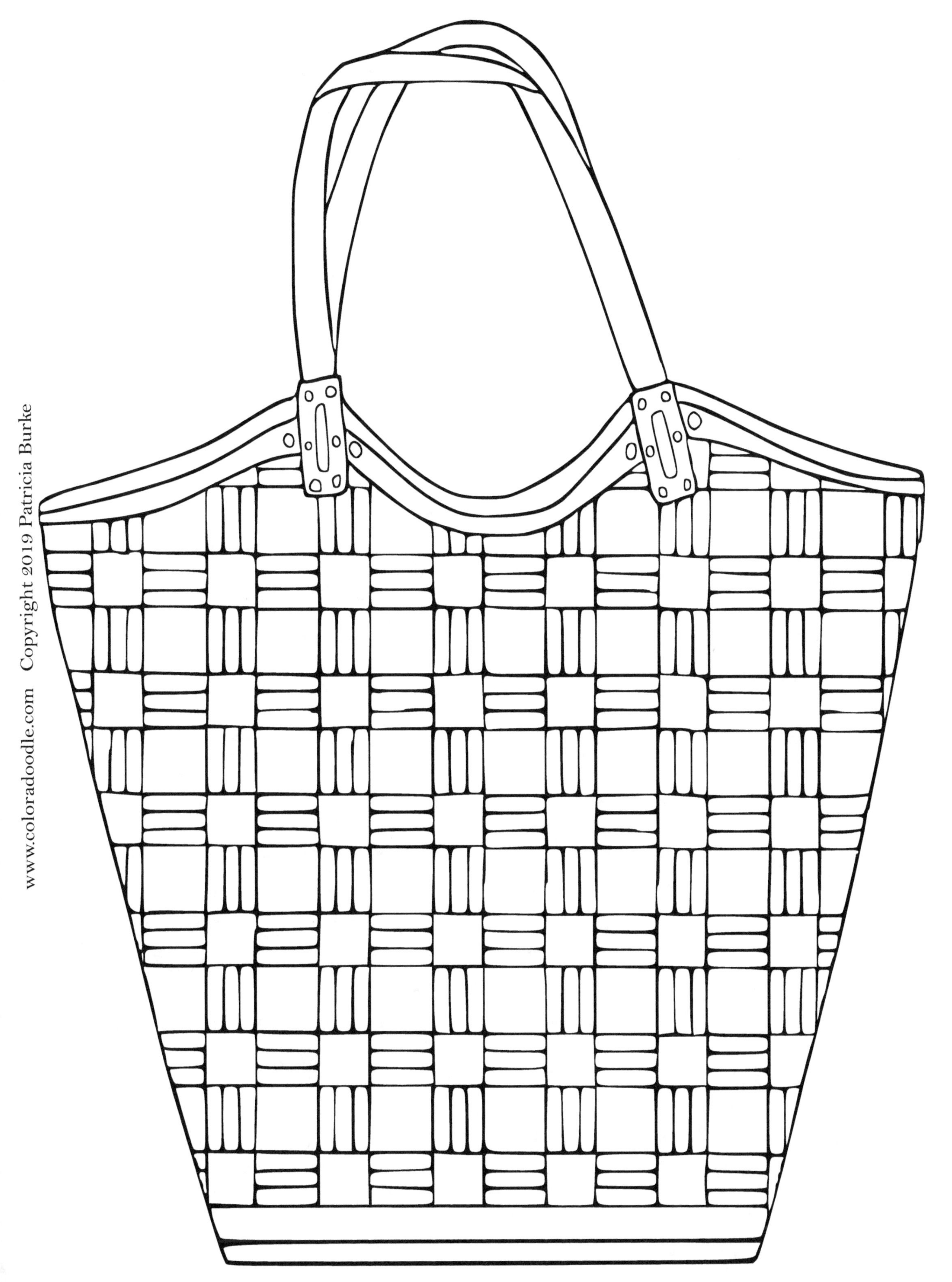

www.coloradoodle.com Copyright 2019 Patricia Burke

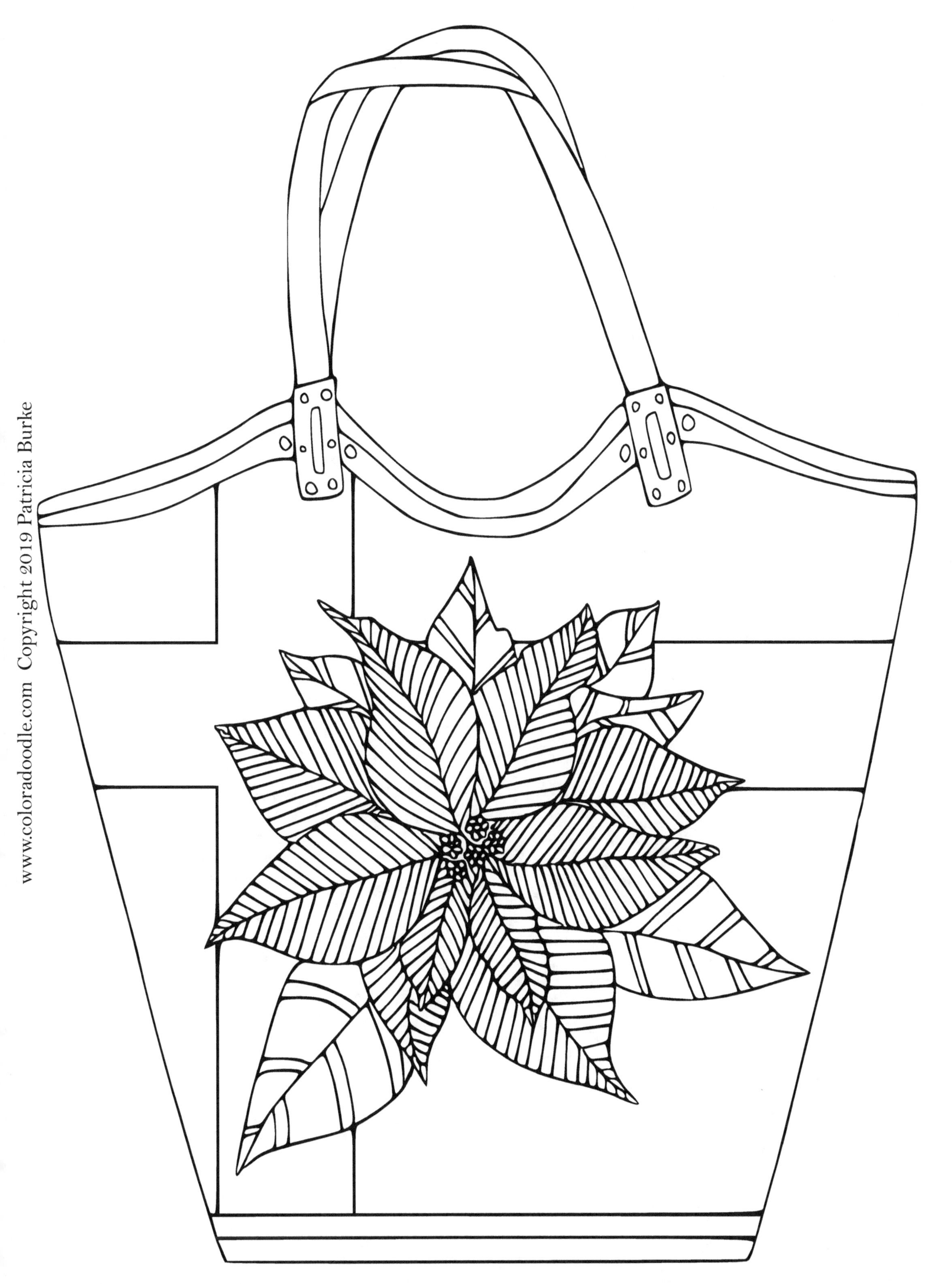

www.coloradoodle.com Copyright 2019 Patricia Burke

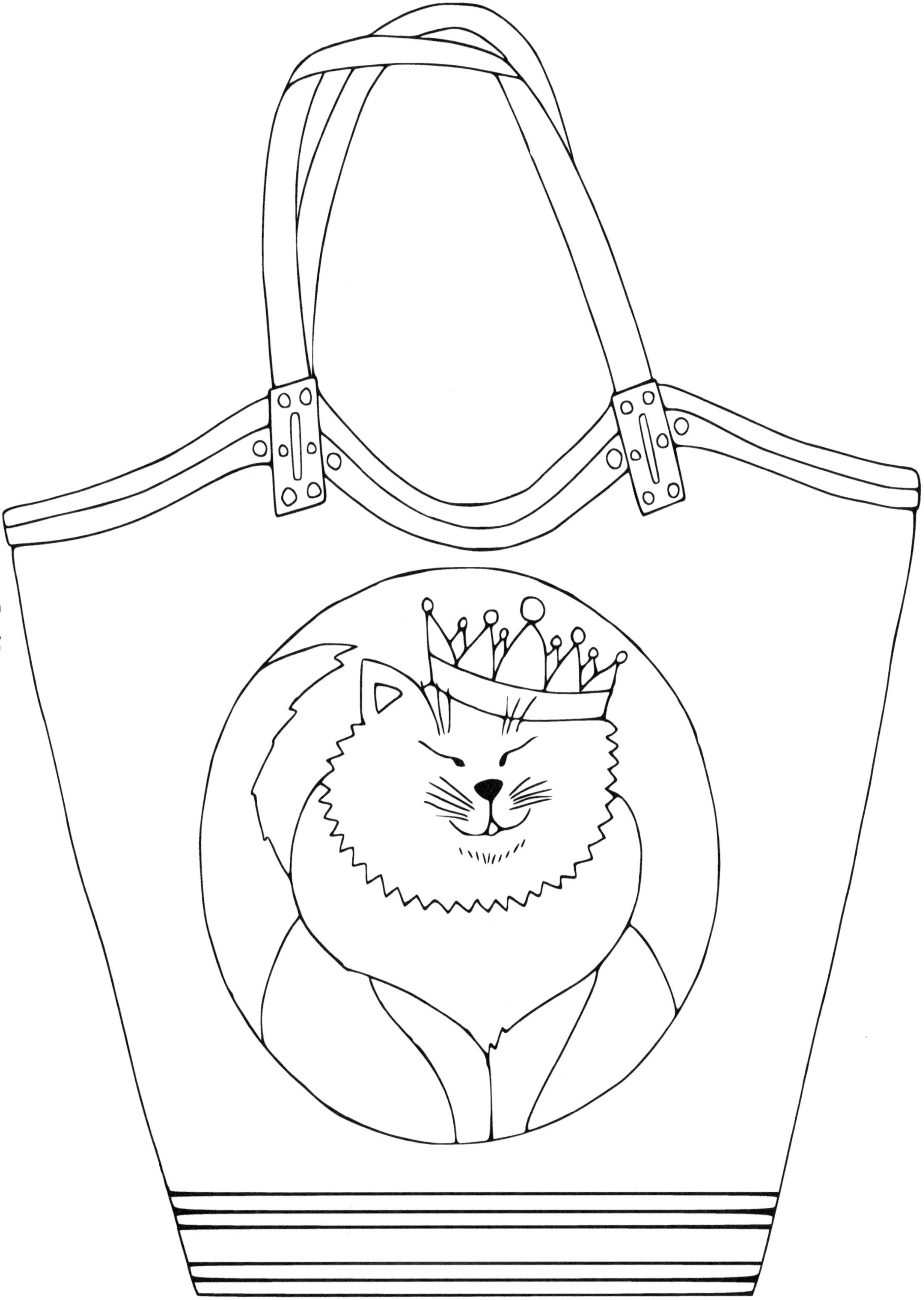

www.coloradoodle.com Copyright 2019 Patricia Burke

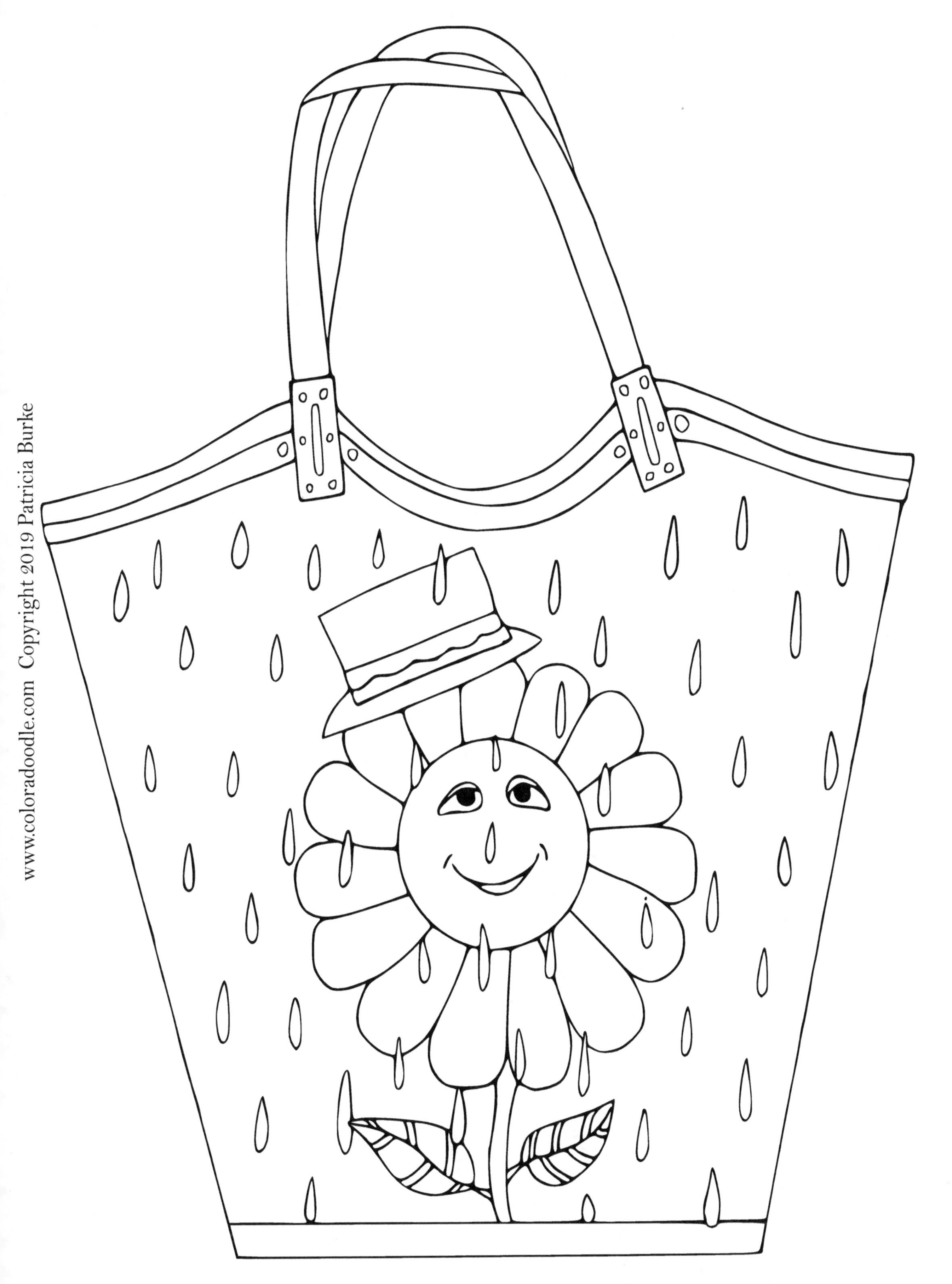

www.coloradoodle.com Copyright 2019 Patricia Burke

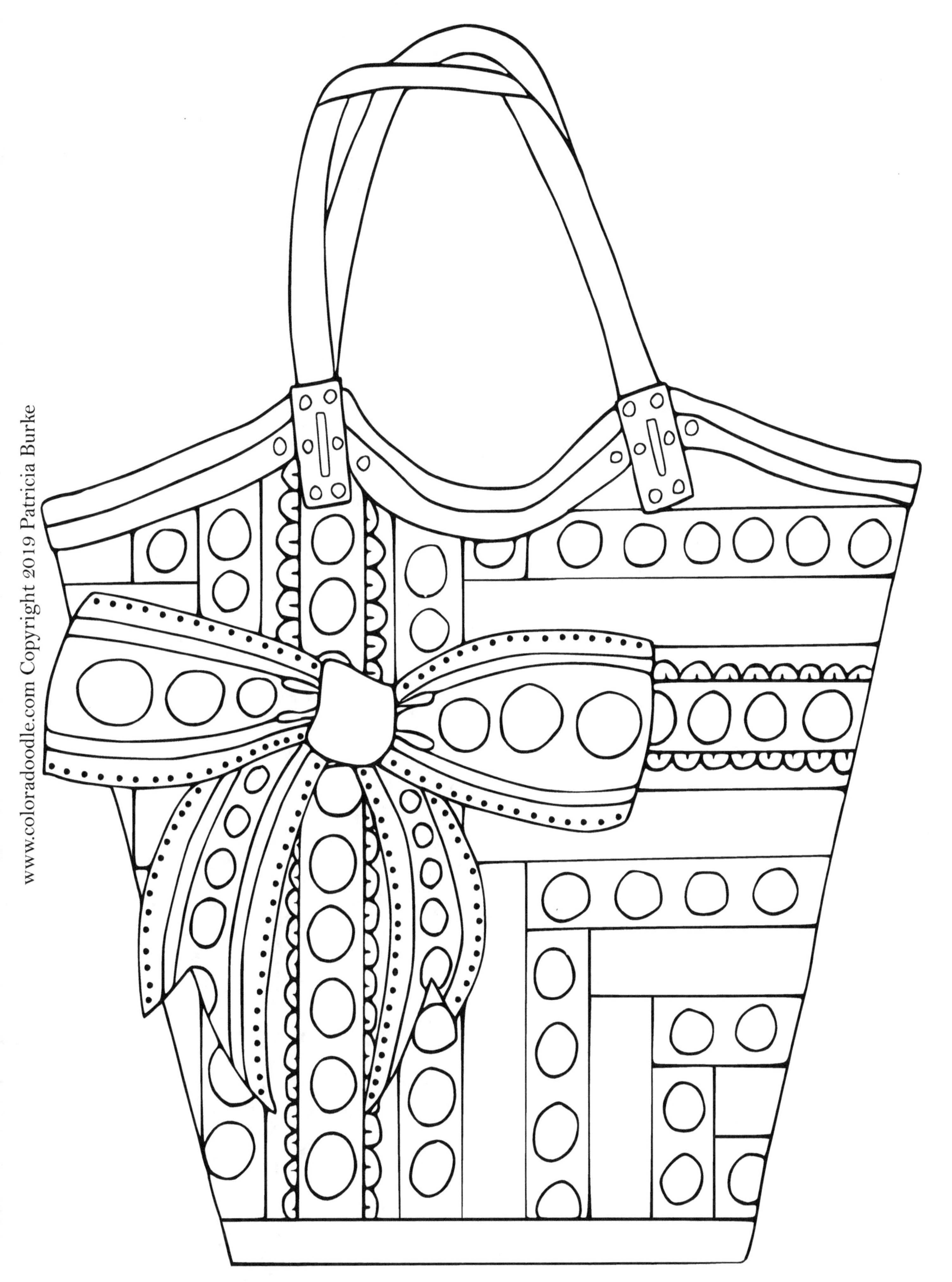

www.coloradoodle.com Copyright 2019 Patricia Burke

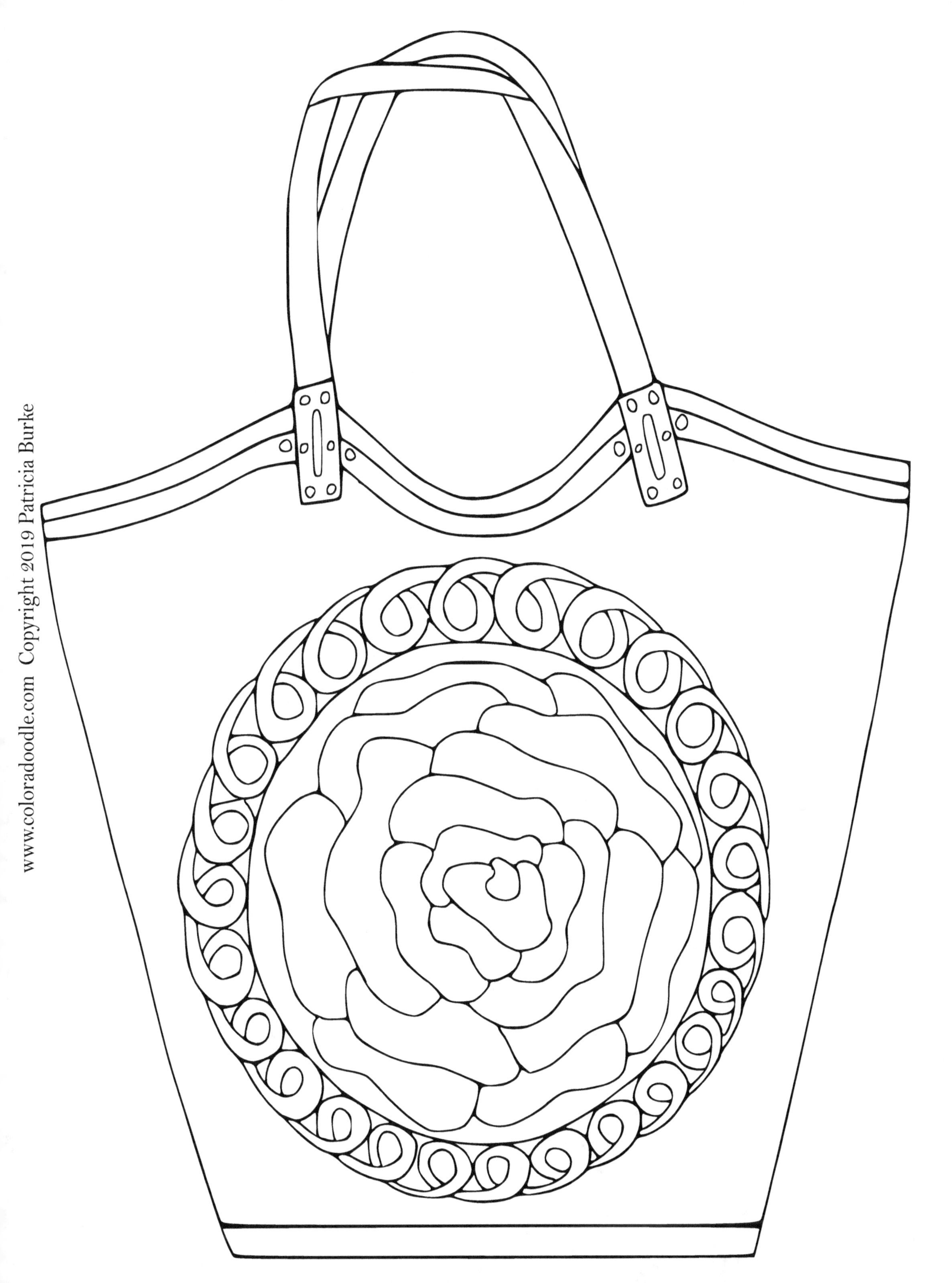

www.coloradoodle.com Copyright 2019 Patricia Burke

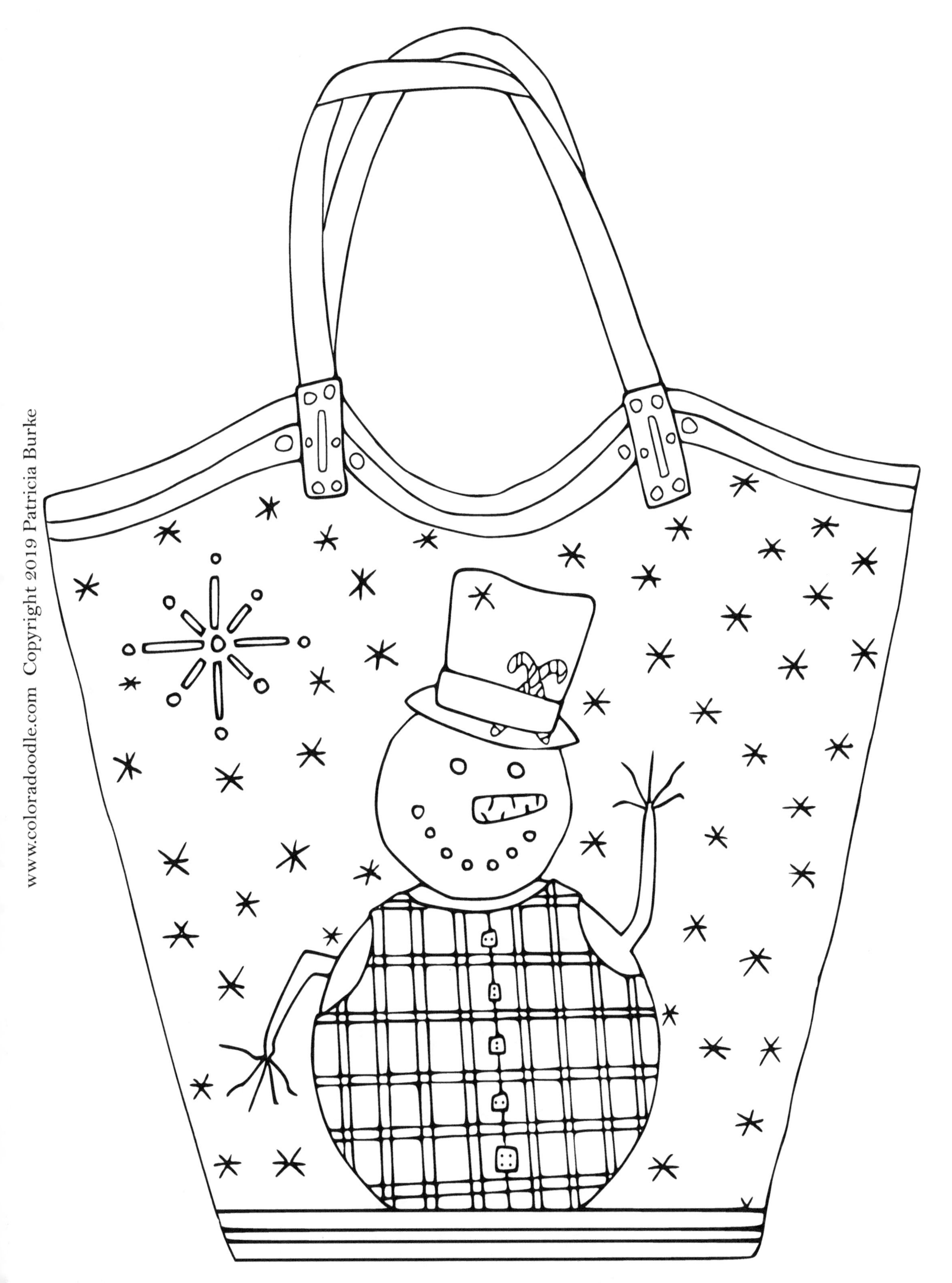

www.coloradoodle.com Copyright 2019 Patricia Burke

www.coloradoodle.com Copyright 2019 Patricia Burke

www.coloradoodle.com Copyright 2019 Patricia Burke

www.coloradoodle.com Copyright 2019 Patricia Burke

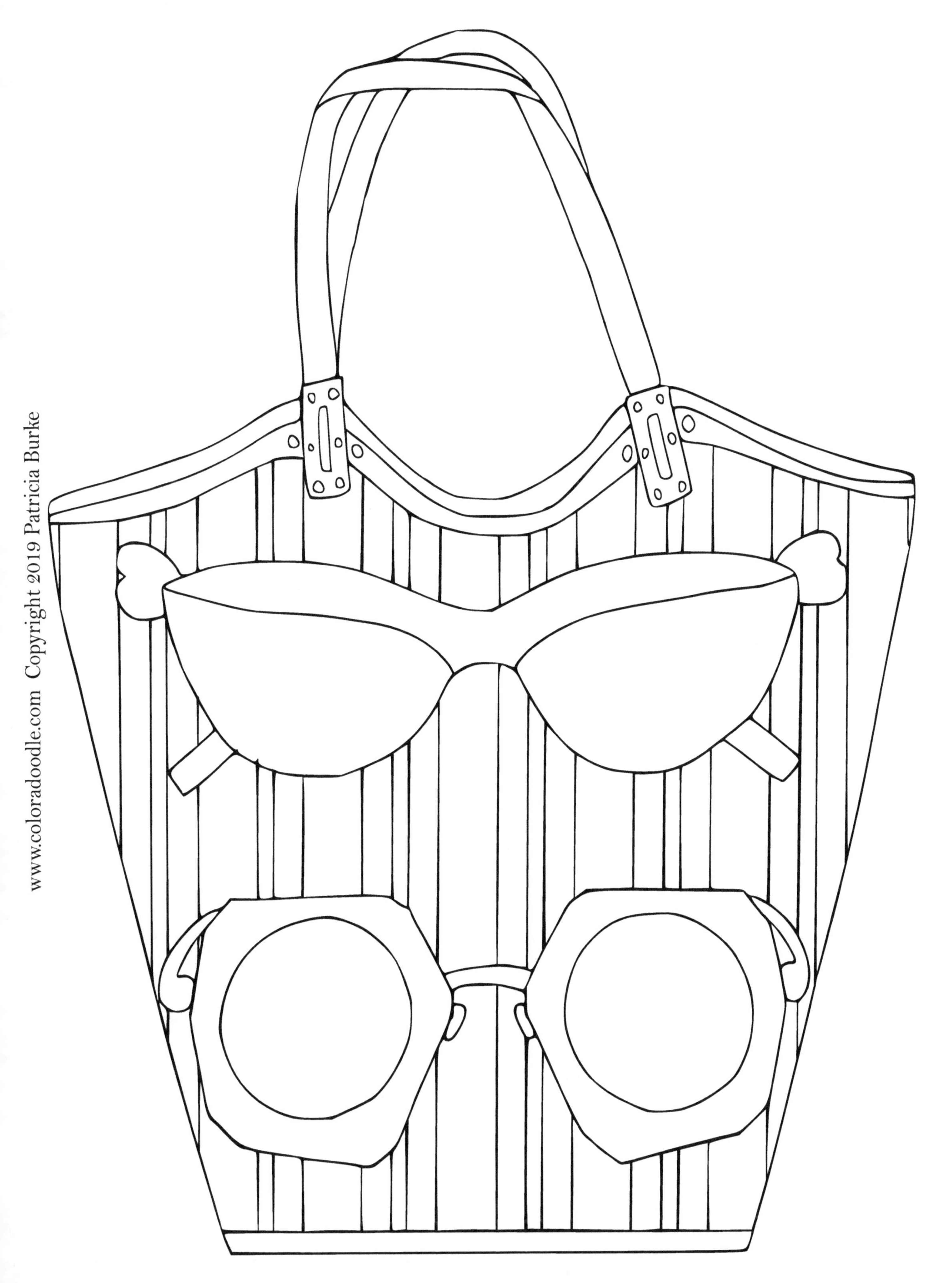

www.coloradoodle.com Copyright 2019 Patricia Burke

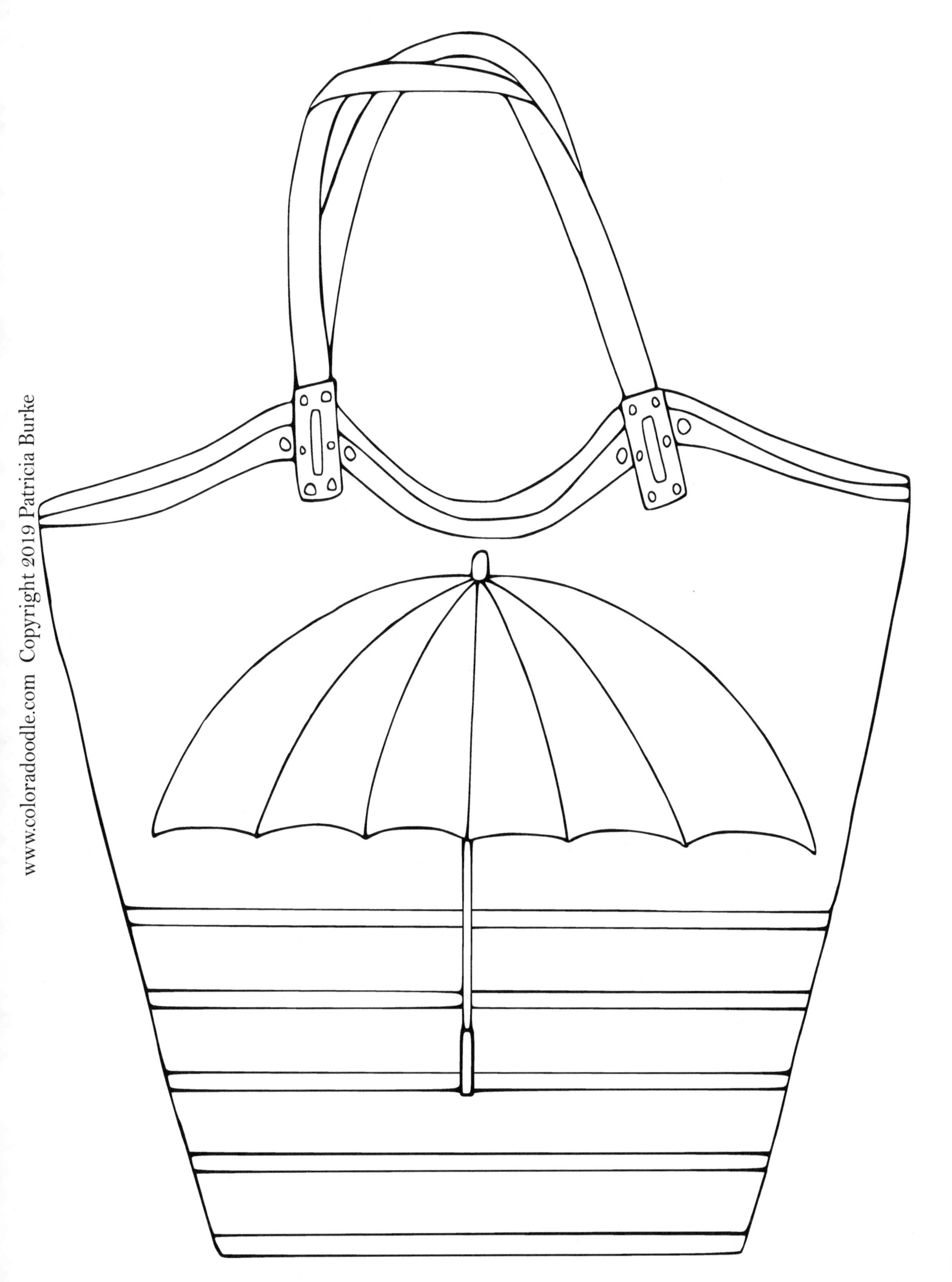
www.coloradoodle.com Copyright 2019 Patricia Burke

www.coloradoodle.com Copyright 2019 Patricia Burke

www.coloradoodle.com Copyright 2019 Patricia Burke

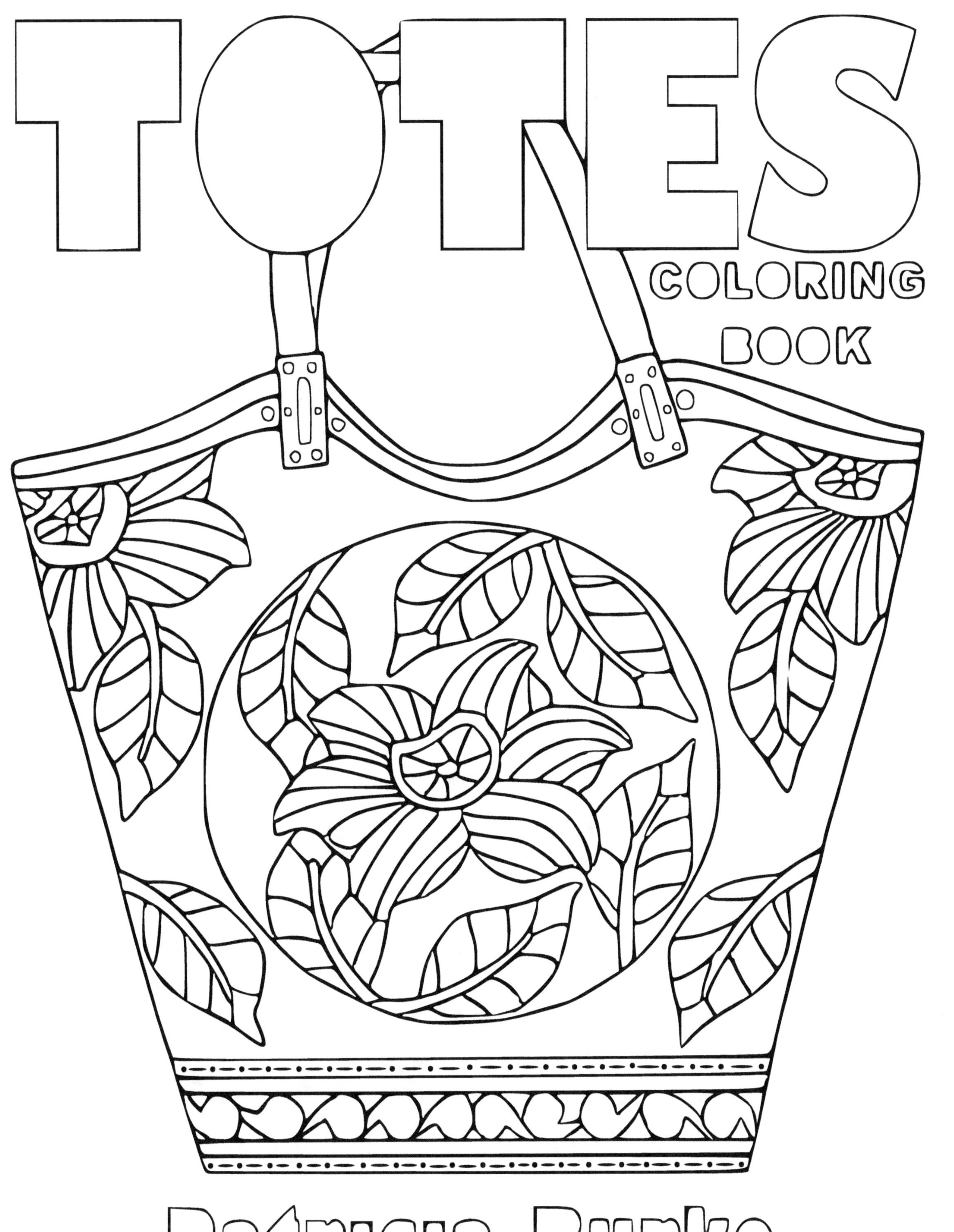

Patricia Burke

www.coloradoodle.com Copyright 2019 Patricia Burke

Design and Color your own TOTE!

www.coloradoodle.com Copyright 2019 Patricia Burke

Design and Color your own TOTE!

www.ingramcontent.com/pod-product-compliance
Lightning Source LLC
LaVergne TN
LVHW080327110826
845155LV00026B/210

* 9 7 8 1 9 5 1 5 7 6 0 2 8 *